# Alfred's
# Easy guitar so...

## MOVIE HITS

Produced by
Alfred Music
P.O. Box 10003
Van Nuys, CA 91410-0003
**alfred.com**

Printed in USA.

ISBN-10: 1-4706-3287-X
ISBN-13: 978-1-4706-3287-8

Cover Photos
Gibson Hummingbird courtesy of Gibson Brands • Duesenberg Dragster DC courtesy of Duesenberg Guitars, USA

 **Alfred Cares.** Contents printed on environmentally responsible paper.

# movie index

# contents

| TITLE | MOVIE | PAGE |
|---|---|---|

4

## STRUM PATTERNS

Below are a number of suggested patterns that may be used while strumming the chords for the songs in this book. Think of these as starting points from which you may embellish, mix up, or create your own patterns.

Note the markings above the staff that indicate the direction of the strums.

⊓ indicates a downstroke

V indicates an upstroke

# FINGERPICKING PATTERNS

Here are some fingerpicking patterns that may be used to arpeggiate chords where indicated in this book.
As with the strum patterns, these are starting points from which you may embellish, mix up, or create your own patterns.

Note the fingerings:
**p** = thumb
**i** = index finger
**m** = middle finger
**a** = ring finger

**Fingerpicking Pattern #1:**

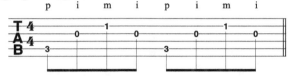

**Fingerpicking Pattern #2:**

**Fingerpicking Pattern #3:**

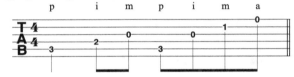

**Fingerpicking Pattern #4:**

**Fingerpicking Pattern #5:**

**Fingerpicking Pattern #6:**

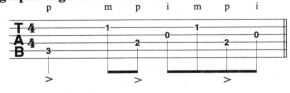

**Fingerpicking Pattern #7:**

**Fingerpicking Pattern #8:**

**Fingerpicking Pattern #9:**

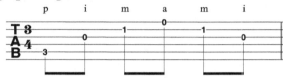

**Fingerpicking Pattern #10:**

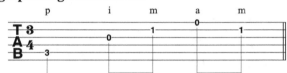

**Fingerpicking Pattern #11:**

**Fingerpicking Pattern #12:**

**Fingerpicking Pattern #13:**

**Fingerpicking Pattern #14:**

**Fingerpicking Pattern #15:**

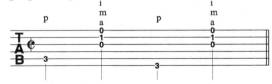

# ARTHUR'S THEME
# (BEST THAT YOU CAN DO)

(from *Arthur*)

Words and Music by
BURT BACHARACH, CAROLE BAYER SAGER,
CHRISTOPHER CROSS and PETER ALLEN

**Use Suggested Strum Pattern #4**

**Moderately** ♩ = 136

1. Once in your life___ you'll find_____ her,     some-one who turns___ your   heart a - round  and
2. Ar - thur, he does___ what   he pleas - es.     All of his life,___   his   mas - ter's toys,   and

Arthur's Theme (Best That You Can Do) - 3 - 1

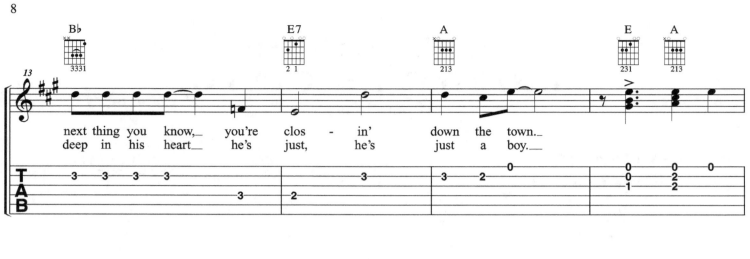

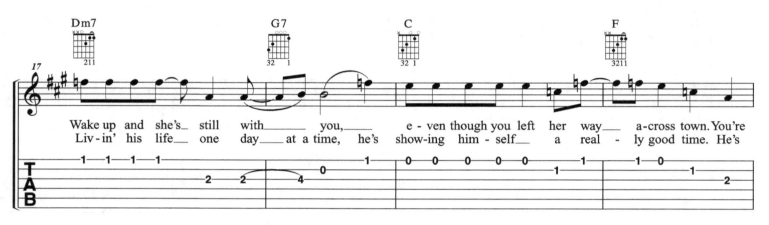

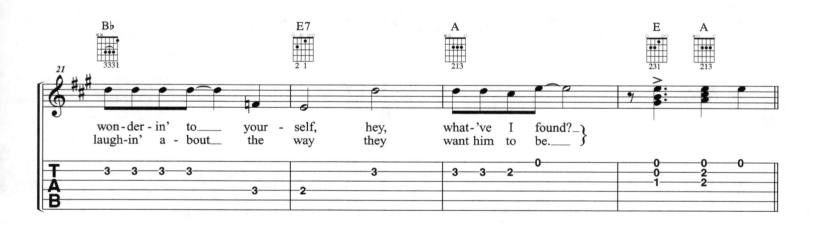

Chorus:

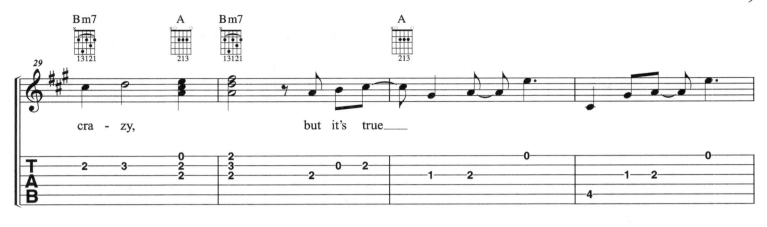

cra - zy, but it's true___

If you get caught be-tween the moon and New York Cit - y,___ the

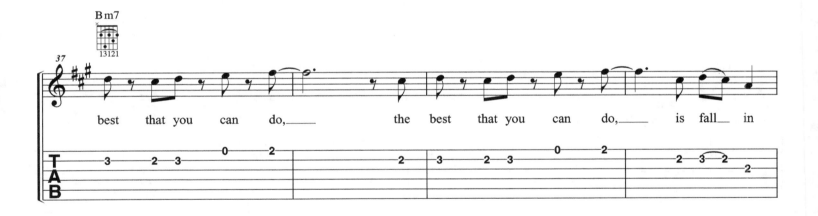

best that you can do,___ the best that you can do,___ is fall__ in

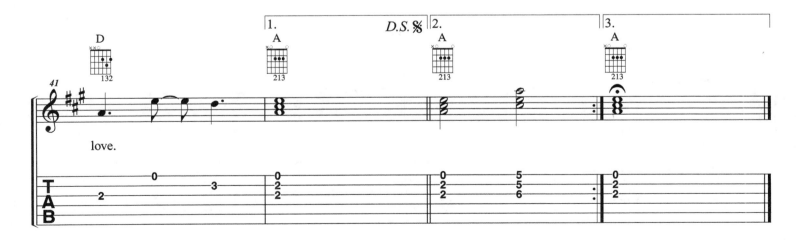

love.

# BECAUSE YOU LOVED ME
## (Theme from *Up Close and Personal*)

Words and Music by
DIANE WARREN

Use Suggested Strum Pattern #1 or #4

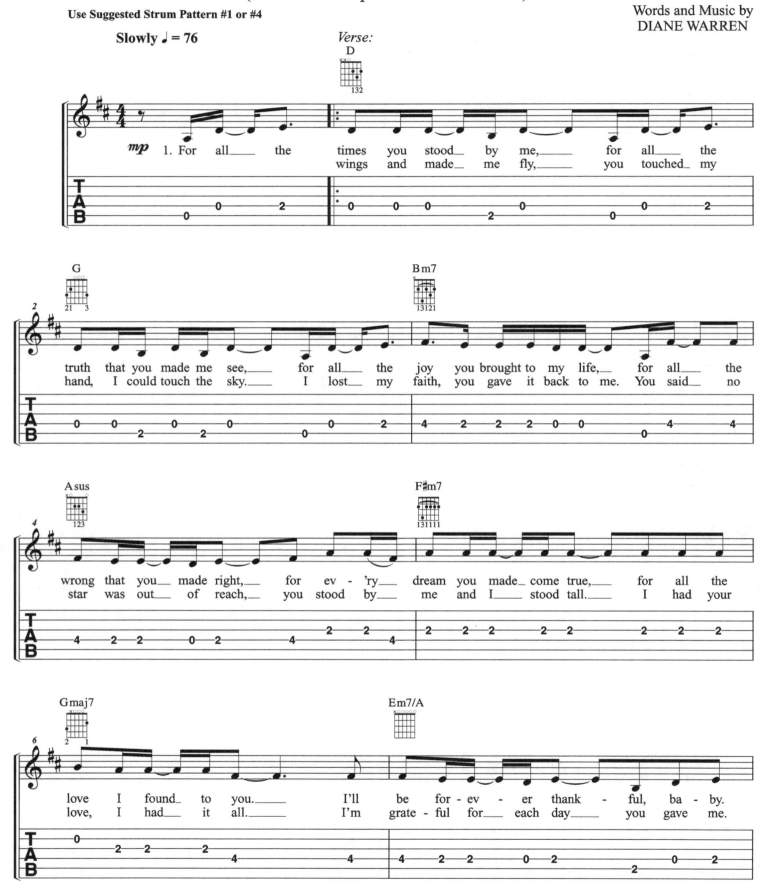

12

1.
Em7/A
D
Em7/A
18
ev - 'ry - thing I am be - cause you loved me.
2. You gave me
2.
Bridge:
D
F#7
Bm
21
loved me.
You were al - ways there for me, the ten - der wind that car - ried me. A
F#7
Bm
24
light in the dark, shin - ing your love in - to my life. You've
Em7
D
26
been my in - spi - ra - tion, through the lies, you were the truth. My
Em7/A
F#m7/B
28
world is a bet - ter place be - cause of you. You were my

# BETTER LOVE

**Use Suggested Strum Pattern #3**
**Moderately**

Words and Music by
A. HOZIER-BYRNE

1. I once kneeled in shak-ing thrill,
2. *See additional lyrics*

I chase the mem-'ry of it still, of ev-'ry chill.

Chid-ed by the si-lence of the hushed sub-lime, blind to the pur-pose of the brute

Di-vine, but you were mine. Star-ing in-to black-ness at some

Better Love - 4 - 1

*Verse 2:*
I have never loved a darker blue,
Than then the darkness I have known in you,
Honed from you.
You whose heart would sing in anarchy,
You who'd laugh at meanings guarantee so beautifully.
When our truth is burned from history,
By those who figure justice in fond memory,
Witness me.
Like fire weeping from a cedar tree,
Know that my love would burn with me or live eternally.
*(To Chorus:)*

# CAN YOU READ MY MIND

(Love Theme from *Superman*)

Words by LESLIE BRICUSSE
Music by JOHN WILLIAMS

**Use Suggested Strum Pattern #1**

**Moderately slow** ♩ = 72

# EVERGREEN
(Love Theme from *A Star Is Born*)

Words by
PAUL WILLIAMS

Music by
BARBRA STREISAND

Evergreen - 3 - 1

# EVERYTHING IS AWESOME
## (Awesome Remixxx!!!)
*(from The Lego Movie)*

Lyrics by
**SHAWN PATTERSON, ANDY SAMBERG,
AKIVA SCHAFFER, JORMA TACCONE,
JOSHUA BARTHOLOMEW and LISA HARRITON**

Music by
**SHAWN PATTERSON**

**Use Suggested Strum Pattern #1**
**Moderately fast**

Everything Is Awesome (Awesome Remixxx!!!) - 5 - 1

24

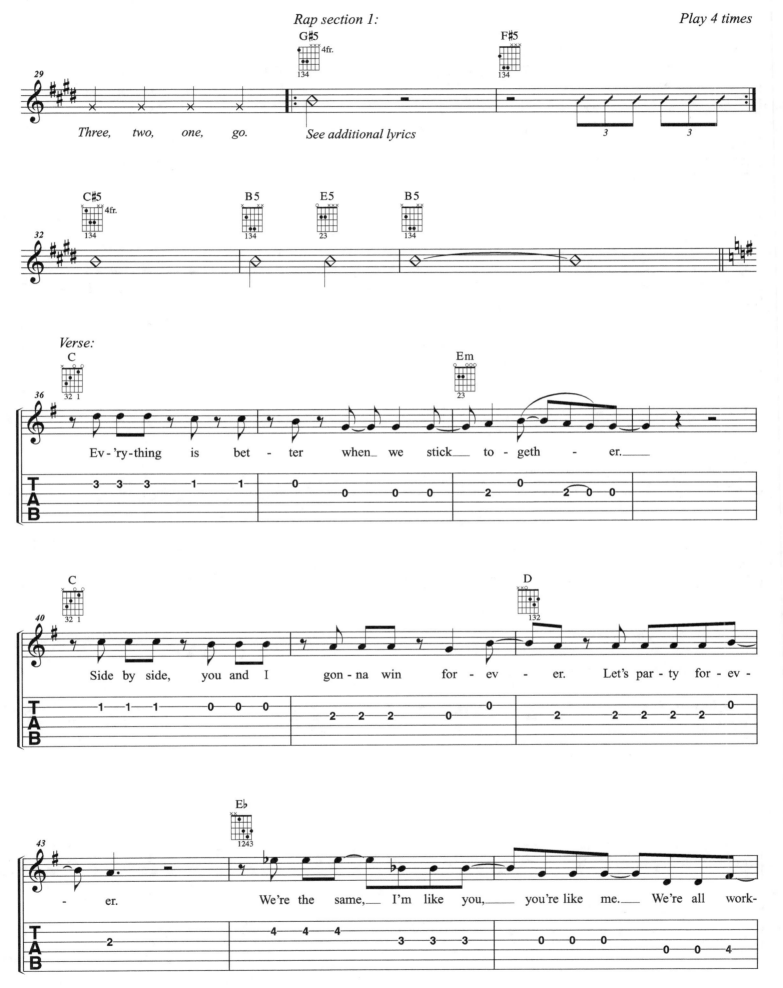

*Rap section 1:*

*Play 4 times*

Three, two, one, go.

*See additional lyrics*

*Verse:*

Ev-'ry-thing is bet - ter when we stick__ to-geth - er.__

Side by side, you and I gon-na win for-ev - er. Let's par-ty for-ev-

- er. We're the same,__ I'm like you,__ you're like me.__ We're all work-

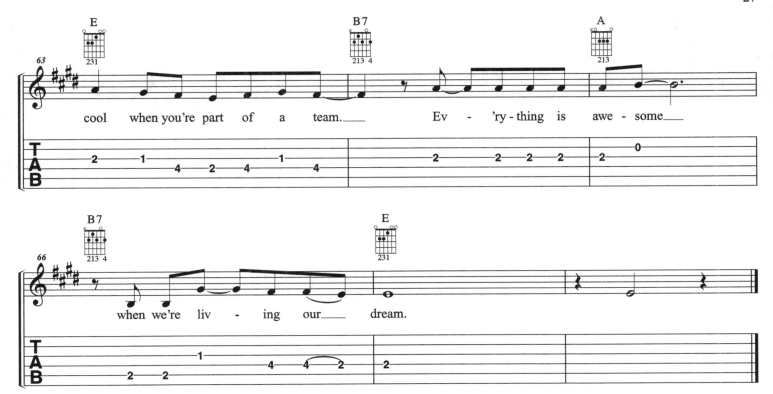

Rap section 1:
Have you heard the news, everyone's talking
Life is good 'cause everything's awesome
Lost my job, it's a new opportunity
More free time for my awesome community.

I feel more awesome than an awesome possum
Dip my body in chocolate frostin'
Three years later, wash off the frostin'
Smellin' like a blossom, everything is awesome
Stepped in mud, got new brown shoes
It's awesome to win, and it's awesome to lose (it's awesome to lose).

Rap section 2:
Blue skies, bouncy springs
We just named two awesome things
A Nobel prize, a piece of string
You know what's awesome? EVERYTHING!

Dogs with fleas, allergies,
A book of Greek antiquities
Brand new pants, a very old vest
Awesome items are the best.

Trees, frogs, clogs
They're awesome
Rocks, clocks, and socks
They're awesome
Figs, and jigs, and twigs
That's awesome
Everything you see, or think, or say
Is awesome.

# (EVERYTHING I DO) I DO IT FOR YOU

Words and Music by
BRYAN ADAMS, ROBERT JOHN "MUTT" LANGE
and MICHAEL KAMEN

Use Suggested Strum Pattern #2

**Slowly** ♩ = 66

(Everything I Do) I Do It for You - 3 - 1

# FALLING SLOWLY

(from *Once*)

Use Suggested Strum Pattern #3

Slowly ♩ = 69

Words and Music by
GLEN HANSARD and MARKETA IRGLOVA

1. I don't know you, but I want you all the more for that. Words fall through me and
2. Fall-ing slow-ly, eyes that know me and I can't go back. Words that take me

al-ways fool me and I can't re-act. Games that nev-er a-
and e-rase me and I'm paint-ed black. Well, you have suf-fered e-

mount to more than they're meant will play them-selves out.
nough and warred with your-self. It's time that you won.

*Chorus:*

Take this sink-in' boat and point it home, we've still got time.

Raise your hope-ful voice, you have a choice, you've made it now.

now. Fall-in' slow-ly, sing your mel-o-dy, I'll sing it loud.

*Outro:*

# FOOTLOOSE

Words by
DEAN PITCHFORD

Music by
KENNY LOGGINS

**Use Suggested Strum Pattern #1**
**(and see Rhy. Gtr. parts in arrangement)**

**Moderately fast**

Verse:

1. Been work-ing    so hard,_    I'm punch-ing_    my card.
2. You're play-ing   so cool,_     o-bey-ing_    ev-'ry rule.

Eight hours___    for what?    Oh, tell me    what I got.___
Dig way down    in your heart.    You're burn-ing,   yearn-ing for some,

Footloose - 6 - 1

*Chorus:*

loose!    Foot - loose.    Kick    off    my    Sun - day    shoes.

Please,    Lou - ise,    pull    me    off    of    my    knees.

Jack,    get    back,    come___ on    be - fore    we    crack.

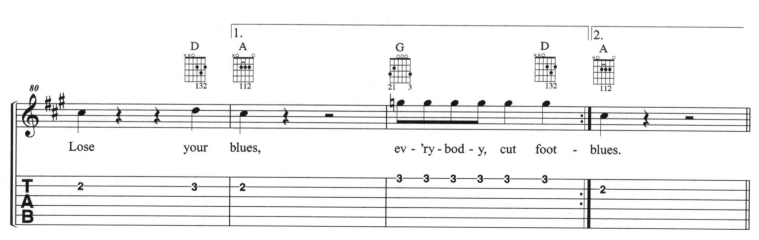

Lose    your    blues,    ev - 'ry - bod - y,    cut    foot - blues.

*Outro:*

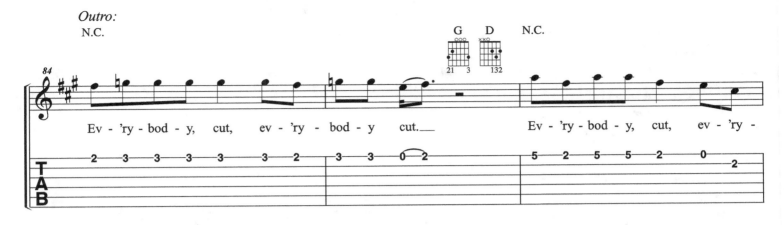

Ev - 'ry - bod - y, cut, ev - 'ry - bod - y cut.___ Ev - 'ry - bod - y, cut, ev - 'ry -

bod - y cut. Ev - 'ry - bod - y, cut, ev - 'ry - bod - y, cut. Ev - 'ry - bod - y,

ev - 'ry - bod - y, cut foot - loose.___

# FOR YOUR EYES ONLY

(from *For Your Eyes Only*)

Lyrics by
MICHAEL LEESON

Music by
BILL CONTI

**Use Suggested Strum Pattern #4**
**Moderately slow** ♩ = 82

For Your Eues Only - 2 - 1

# GHOSTBUSTERS

Words and Music by
RAY PARKER, JR.

**Use Suggested Strum Pattern #4**

**Moderately**

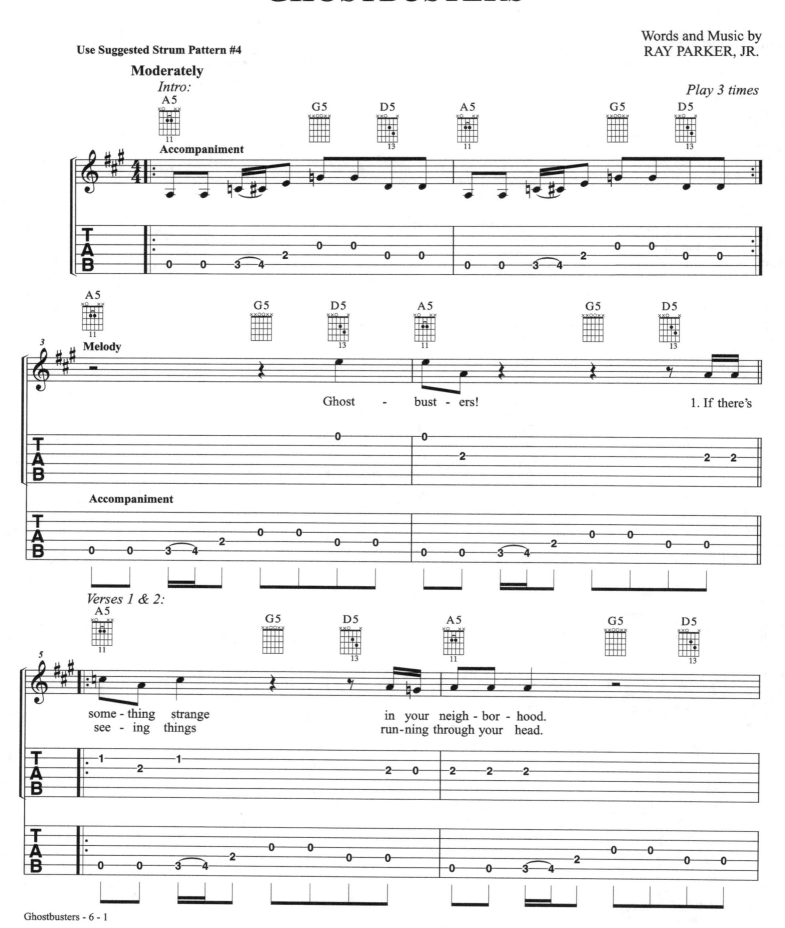

Ghost - bust - ers!

1. If there's

some - thing strange
see - ing things

in your neigh - bor - hood.
run - ning through your head.

Ghostbusters - 6 - 1

44

I ain't 'fraid— of no ghost!

I ain't 'fraid— of no ghost!

*To Coda* ⊕

1.

2. If you're

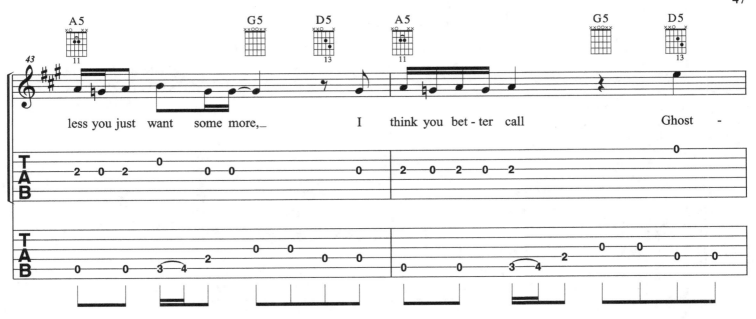

less you just want some more,_ I think you bet - ter call Ghost -

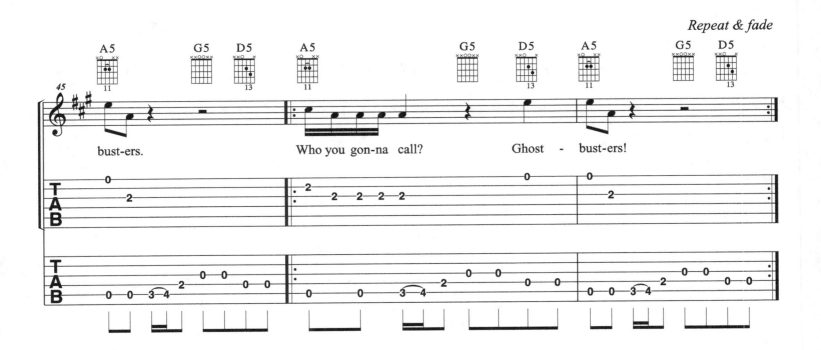

*Repeat & fade*

bust-ers. Who you gon-na call? Ghost - bust-ers!

Verse 3:
Who you gonna call?
Ghostbusters!
If you've had a dose of a freaky ghost,
Baby, you'd better call…
Ghostbusters!
Let me tell you something,
Bustin' makes me feel good.
I ain't afraid of no ghost.
I ain't afraid of no ghost.
*(To Coda)*

# GLORY OF LOVE
### (Theme from *The Karate Kid, Part II*)

Words and Music by
DAVID FOSTER, PETER CETERA
and DIANE NINI

1. To-night it's ver-y clear, as we're both stand-ing here, there's so man-y things I
2.3. *See additional lyrics*

want to say. I will al-ways love you,___ I will nev-er leave you a-

lone.

Glory of Love - 4 - 1

Glory of Love - 4 - 2

*Verse 2:*
Sometimes I just forget, say things I might regret,
It breaks my heart to see you crying.
I don't want to lose you,
I could never make it alone.
*(To Chorus:)*

*Verse 3:*
You keep me standing tall, you help me through it all,
I'm always strong when you're beside me.
I have always needed you,
I could never make it alone.
*(To Chorus:)*

# GOLDFINGER

Lyrics by
**LESLIE BRICUSSE** and
**ANTHONY NEWLEY**

Music by
**JOHN BARRY**

**Use Suggested Strum Pattern #6**
**Moderately**

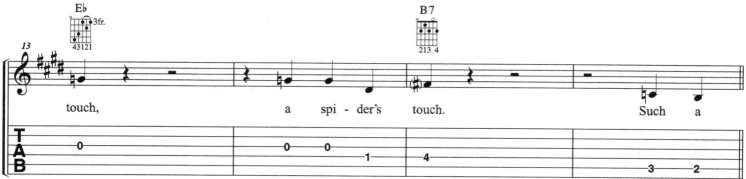

Goldfinger - 3 - 1

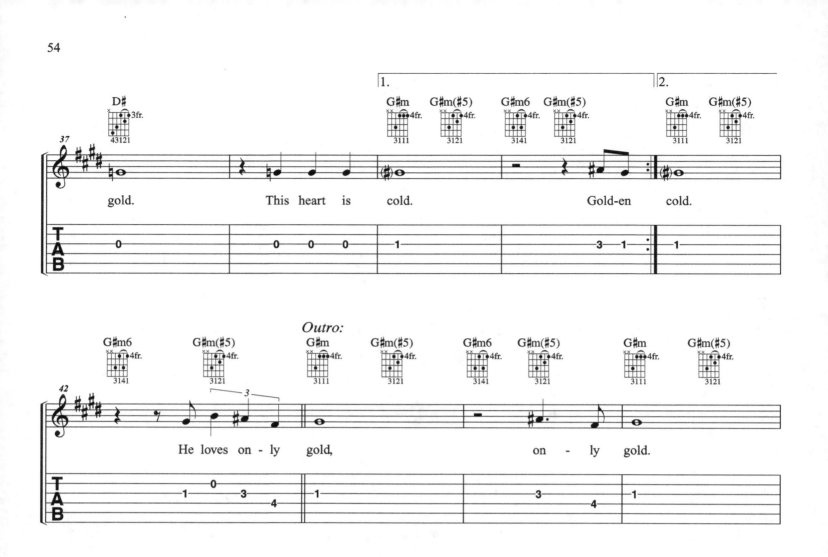

Outro:

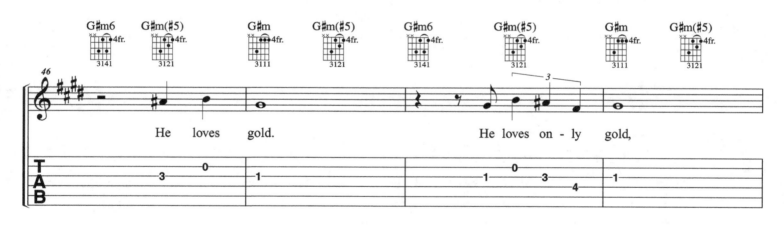

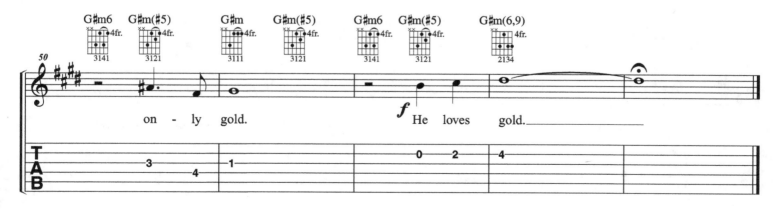

# THE GOOD, THE BAD AND THE UGLY

## (Main Title)

By
ENNIO MORRICONE

**Use Suggested Strum Pattern #7**
**Western gallop**

The Good, the Bad and the Ugly - 3 - 1

The Good, the Bad and the Ugly - 3 - 2

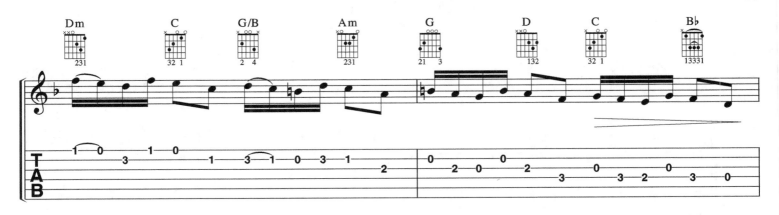

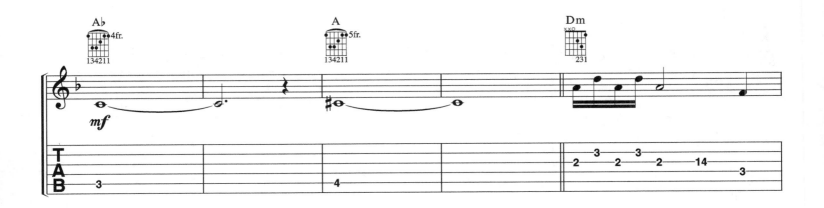

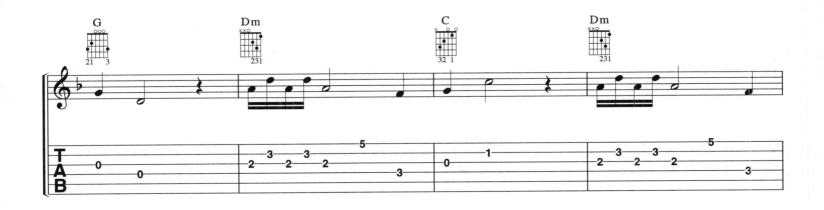

The Good, the Bad and the Ugly - 3 - 3

# GONNA FLY NOW
### (Theme from *Rocky*)

Words and Music by
BILL CONTI, AYN ROBBINS
and CAROL CONNERS

**Use Suggested Strum Pattern #2**
**Moderately fast**

Gonna Fly Now - 2 - 1

# THE GREAT ESCAPE MARCH

Words by
**AL STILLMAN**

Music by
ELMER BERNSTEIN

**Use Suggested Strum Pattern #14**

The Great Escape March - 2 - 1

The Great Escape March - 2 - 2

# THE GREATEST LOVE OF ALL

Words by
LINDA CREED

Music by
MICHAEL MASSER

# HIGH NOON
## (Do Not Forsake Me, Oh My Darlin')
## Main Title

Words by
NED WASHINGTON

Music by
DIMITRI TIOMKIN

**Use Intro as suggested strum pattern**
**Moderate cut time**

*Chorus 1:*

Do not for - sake me, oh my dar - lin'._____ On this our

wed - ding day._____ Do not for - sake me, oh my

dar - lin'. Wait,_____ wait a - long._____

𝄋 *Chorus 2 & 3:*

2. I do not know what fate a - waits me._____ I on - ly
3. Do not for - sake me, oh my dar - lin'. You made that

High Noon - 3 - 1

# I DON'T WANT TO MISS A THING

(from *Armageddon*)

Use Suggested Strum Pattern #1

Words and Music by
DIANE WARREN

I Don't Want to Miss a Thing - 3 - 1

# I LOVE TO SEE YOU SMILE

(from *Parenthood*)

Use Suggested Strum Pattern #14

Words and Music by
RANDY NEWMAN

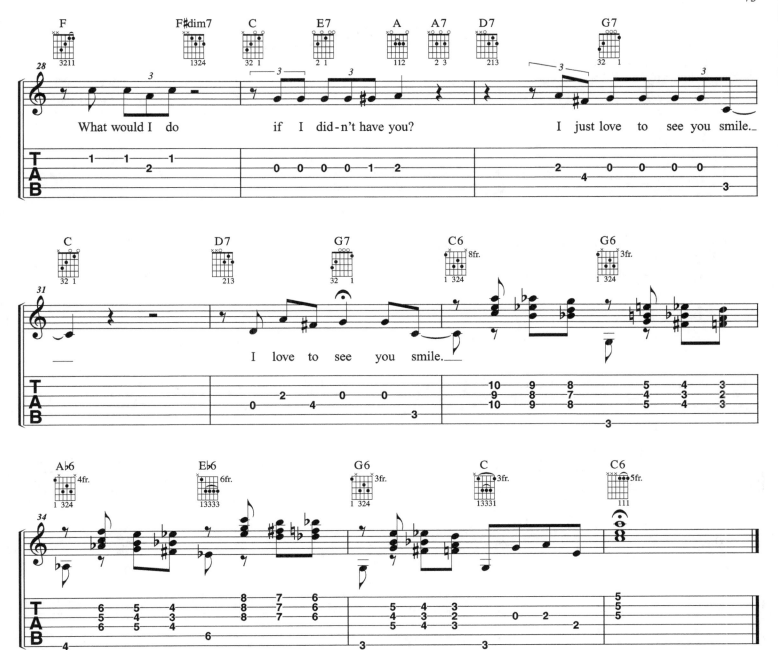

*Verse 2:*
Don't want to take a trip to China.
Don't want to sail up the Nile.
Wouldn't want to get too far from where you are
'Cause I love to see you smile.

*Verse 3:*
(Instrumental)

*Verse 4:*
Like a sink without a faucet,
Like a watch without a dial,
What would I do if I didn't have you?
I love to see you smile.
(To Bridge:)

# I SEE FIRE

**Use Suggested Strum Pattern #6
or Fingerpicking Pattern #6**

Words and Music by
ED SHEERAN

I See Fire - 6 - 1

78

I See Fire - 6 - 5

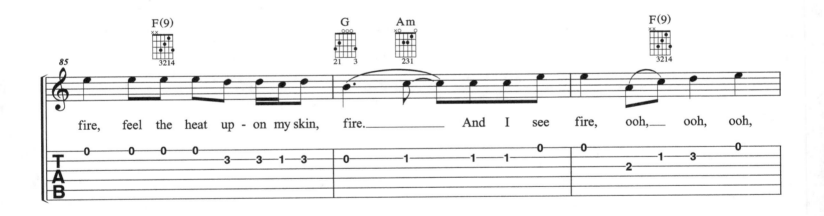

I See Fire - 6 - 6

# IF I ONLY HAD A BRAIN

(from *The Wizard of Oz*)

Lyrics by
E.Y. HARBURG

Music by
HAROLD ARLEN

**Use Suggested Strum Pattern #14**

**Moderate swing**

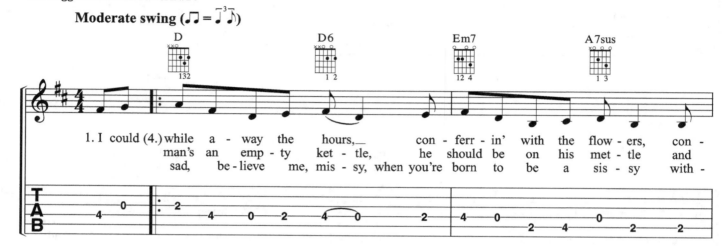

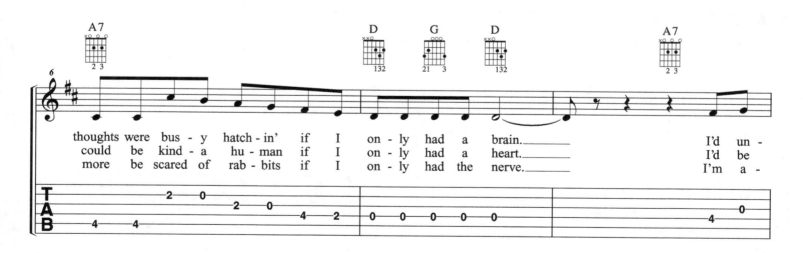

If I Only Had a Brain - 3 - 1

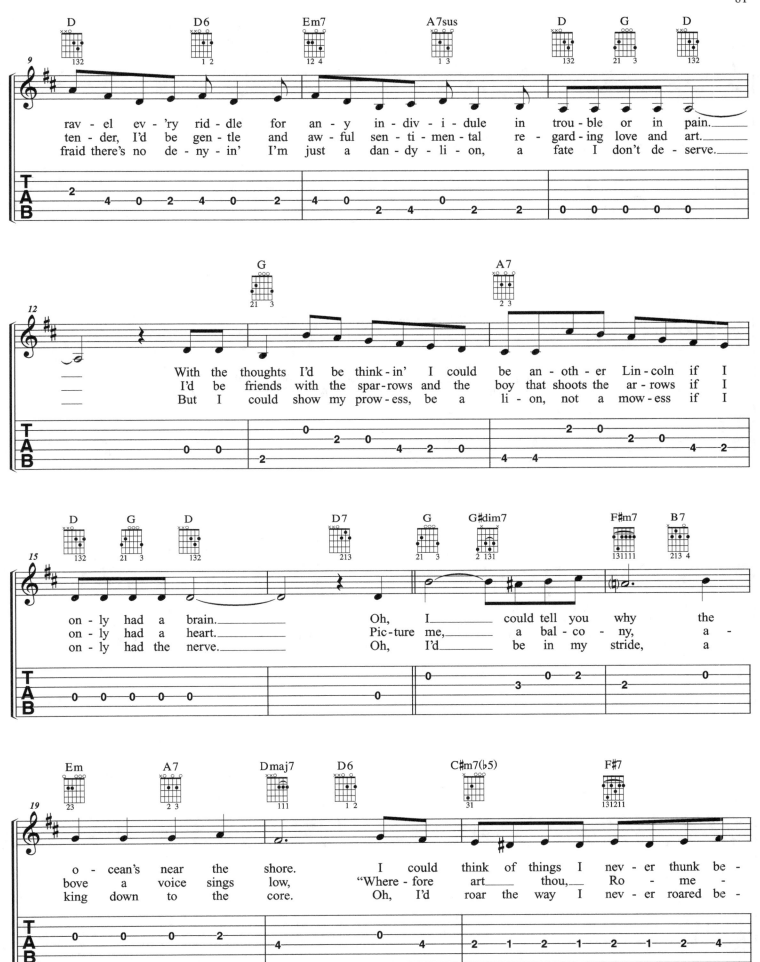

# IT MIGHT BE YOU
## (Theme from *Tootsie*)

Words by
ALAN and MARILYN BERGMAN

Music by
DAVE GRUSIN

**Use Suggested Strum Pattern #6**
**Moderately** ♩ = 90

It Might Be You - 3 - 1

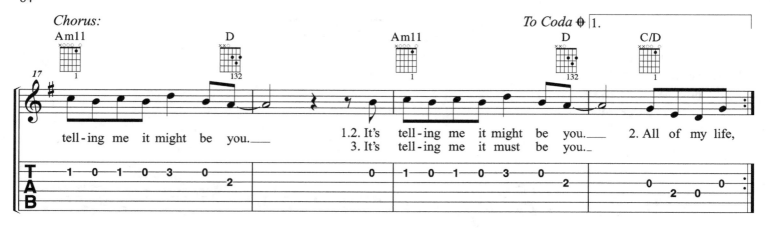

*Chorus:*

telling me it might be you.___

1.2. It's telling me it might be you.___    2. All of my life,
3. It's telling me it must be you.___

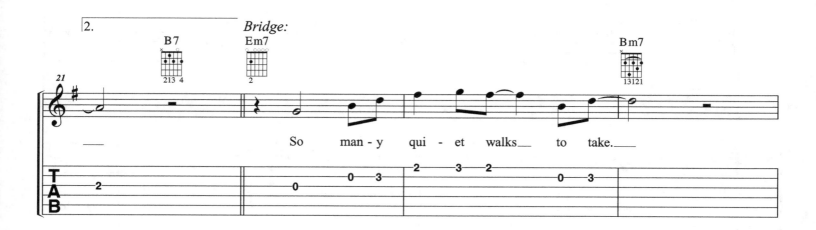

*Bridge:*

___    So man-y qui-et walks___ to take.___

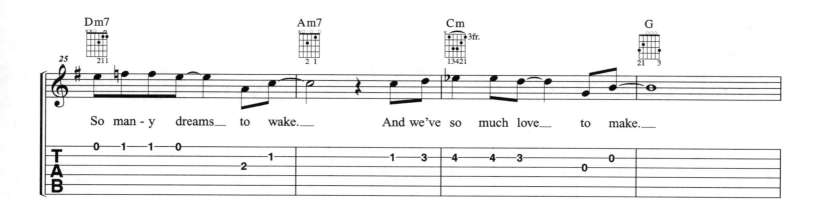

So man-y dreams___ to wake.___    And we've so much love___ to make.___

I think we're gon-na need___ some time.___    May-be

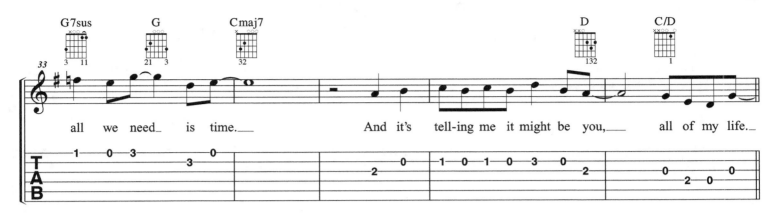

all we need___ is time.___ And it's tell-ing me it might be you,___ all of my life.___

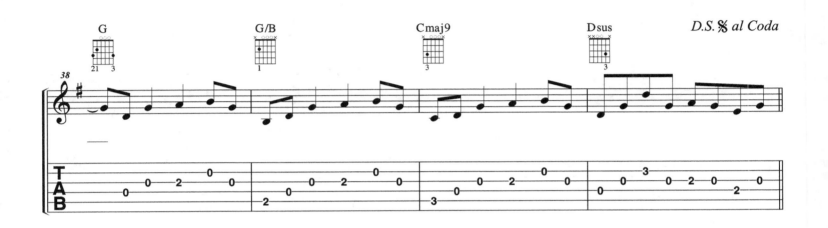

*D.S. 𝄋 al Coda*

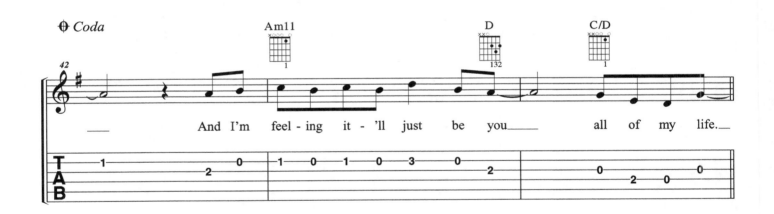

⊕ *Coda*

___ And I'm feel-ing it - 'll just be you___ all of my life.___

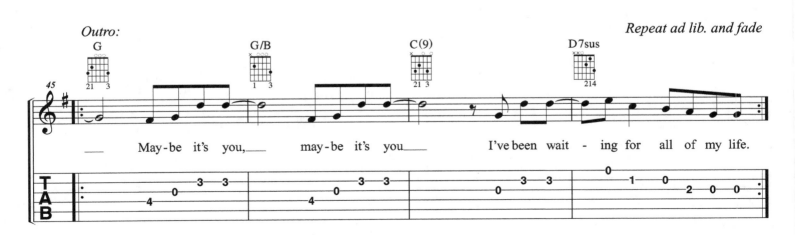

*Outro:*

*Repeat ad lib. and fade*

___ May-be it's you,___ may-be it's you___ I've been wait - ing for all of my life.

It Might Be You - 3 - 3

# IN DREAMS

(from *The Lord of the Rings: The Fellowship of the Ring*)

Use Suggested Strum Pattern #2
or Fingerpicking Pattern #5
**Slowly and freely**

Words and Music by
FRAN WALSH and HOWARD SHORE

In Dreams - 2 - 1

# INTO THE WEST

(from *The Lord of the Rings: The Return of the King*)

**Use Suggested Strum Pattern #6
or Fingerpicking Pattern #4**

Words and Music by
HOWARD SHORE, FRAN WALSH
and ANNIE LENNOX

Lay___ down___                    your sweet and wea-ry head.

Night is fall-ing.___      You have come to jour-ney's end.

Sleep___ now.    Dream    of the ones who came be-fore.

They are call-ing        from a-cross the dis-tant shore.

Into the West - 4 - 1

# JAMES BOND THEME

By MONTY NORMAN

**Use Suggested Strum Pattern #1 (all downstrokes)**

**Moderately fast**

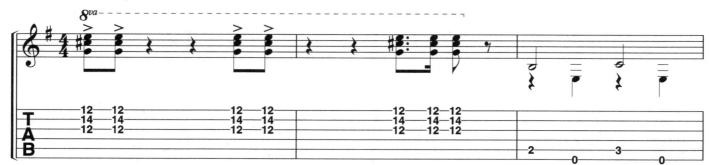

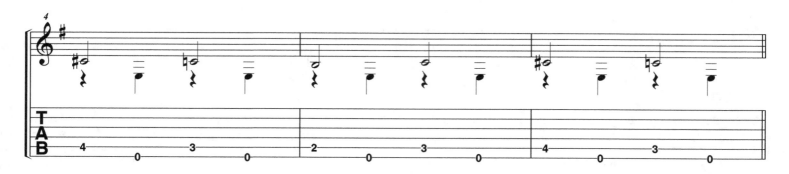

Jmaes Bond Theme - 3 - 1

**Swing feel**

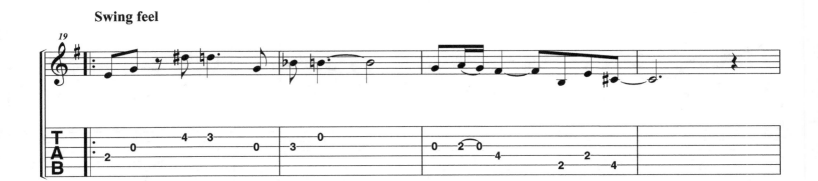

**Moderately fast**

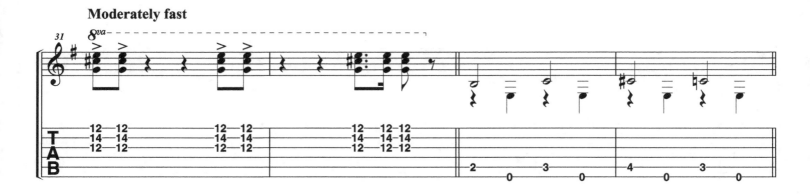

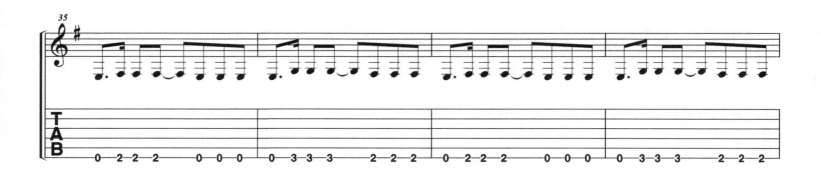

N.C.

Em(maj9)

# LET IT GO

## (from Walt Disney's *Frozen*)

**Use Suggested Strum Pattern #6**
**Moderately, with a half-time feel**

Music and Lyrics by
KRISTEN ANDERSON-LOPEZ
and ROBERT LOPEZ

*Verse 1:*

The snow glows white on the moun-tain to - night, not a foot-print to be seen.

king-dom of i - so - la - tion, and it looks like I'm the queen.

The wind is howl - ing like this swirl-ing storm in - side.

Could-n't keep it in, heav - en knows I've tried.

Don't let them in, don't let them see. Be the good girl you al-ways have to be.

Let It Go - 5 - 1

Play B note on D.S. only.

Interlude:

Bridge:

# MAMMA MIA

Words and Music by
BENNY ANDERSSON, STIG ANDERSON
and BJORN ULVAEUS

**Use Suggested Strum Pattern #1**
**Moderately bright**

*Verse:*

1. I've been cheat-ed by you___ since I don't_ know when.___
2. I've been an-gry and sad___ a-bout things that_ you do.___

So I made up my mind___ it must come to an end.___
I can't count all the times___ that I've told you we're through.___

Look at me now,___ will I ev-er learn?
And when you go,___ when you slam the door,

Mamma Mia - 4 - 1

# MIDNIGHT COWBOY

**Use Suggested Strum Pattern #13**

**Moderately slow**

N.C.

By
JOHN BARRY

Midnight Cowboy - 2 - 1

# THE MAGNIFICENT SEVEN

(from *The Magnificent Seven*)

By
ELMER BERNSTEIN

Use Suggested Strum Pattern #6
**Brightly**

The Magnificent Seven - 3 - 1

# NEVER ON SUNDAY

Lyrics by
BILLY TOWNE

Music by
MANOS HADJIDAKIS

**Use Suggested Strum Pattern #14
or Fingerpicking Pattern #15**

**Moderately bright**

Oh, you can kiss me on a

*Chorus:*

Mon - day, a Mon - day, a Mon - day is ver - y, ver - y good.

Or you can kiss me on a

Tues - day, a Tues - day, a Tues - day, in fact I wish you would.

Or you can kiss me on a

Wednes - day, a Thurs - day, a Fri - day and Sat - ur - day is best.

But nev - er, nev - er on a

Never on Sunday - 3 - 1

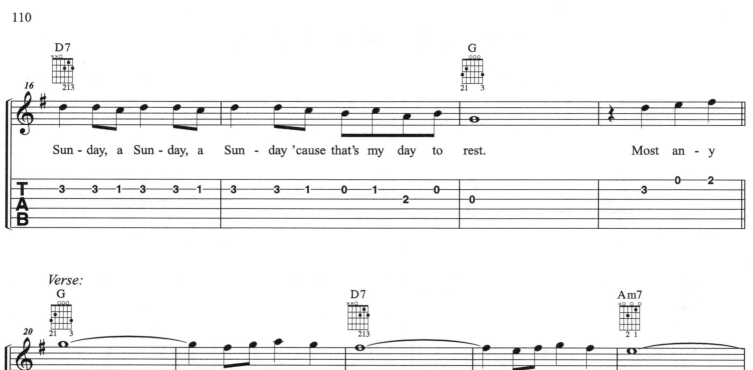

Sun - day, a Sun - day, a Sun - day 'cause that's my day to rest.  Most an - y

*Verse:*

day_____ you can be my guest,_____ an - y day you say,_____

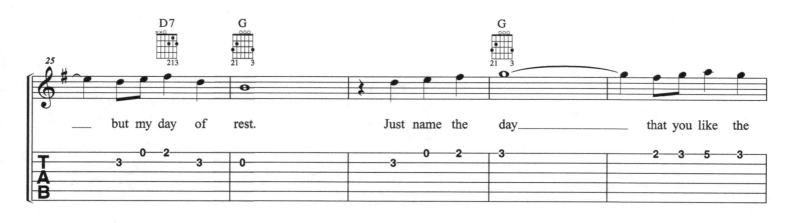

___ but my day of rest.  Just name the day_____ that you like the

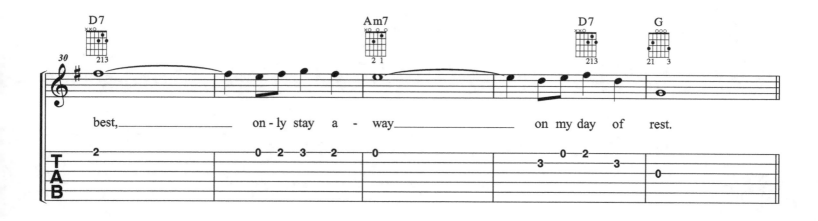

best,_____ on - ly stay a - way_____ on my day of rest.

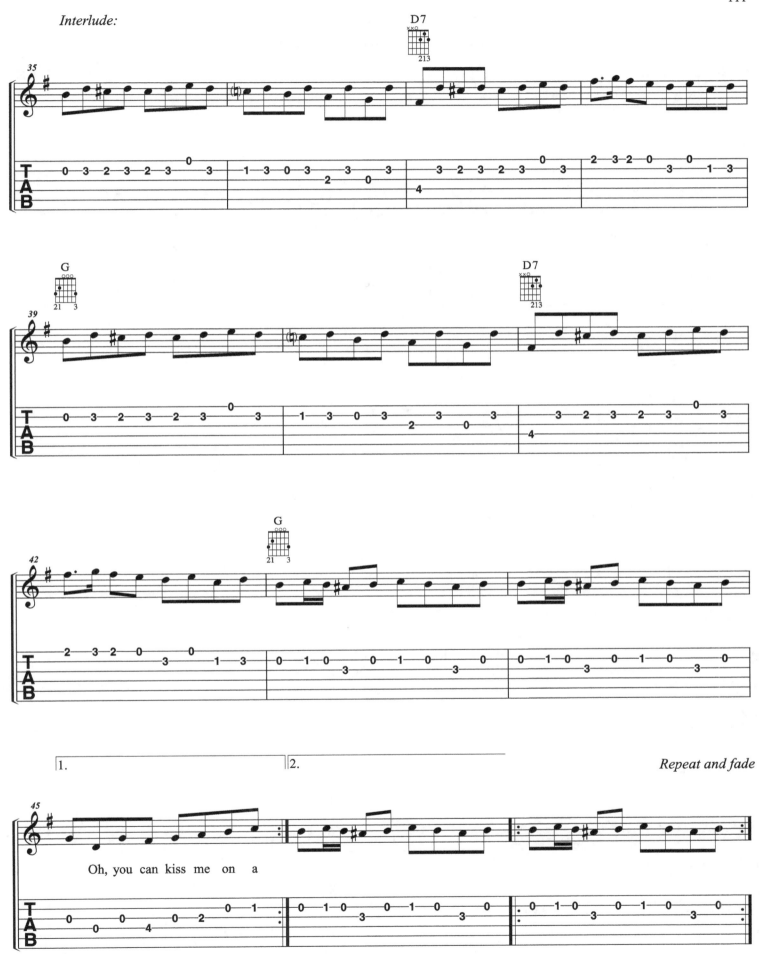

Oh, you can kiss me on a

# NOBODY DOES IT BETTER

(from *The Spy Who Loved Me*)

Lyrics by
CAROLE BAYER SAGER

Music by
MARVIN HAMLISCH

# THE NOTEBOOK
## (Main Title)

**Use Suggested Strum Pattern #14
or Fingerpicking Pattern #4**

Written by
AARON ZIGMAN

**Slowly with expression**

The Notebook - 2 - 1

# OVER THE RAINBOW
### (from *The Wizard of Oz*)

Lyrics by
E.Y. HARBURG

Music by
HAROLD ARLEN

**Use Suggested Strum Pattern #3
or Fingerpicking Pattern #1**

# THE PINK PANTHER

(from *The Pink Panther*)

By
HENRY MANCINI

**Use Suggested Strum Pattern #3**

**Moderate swing**

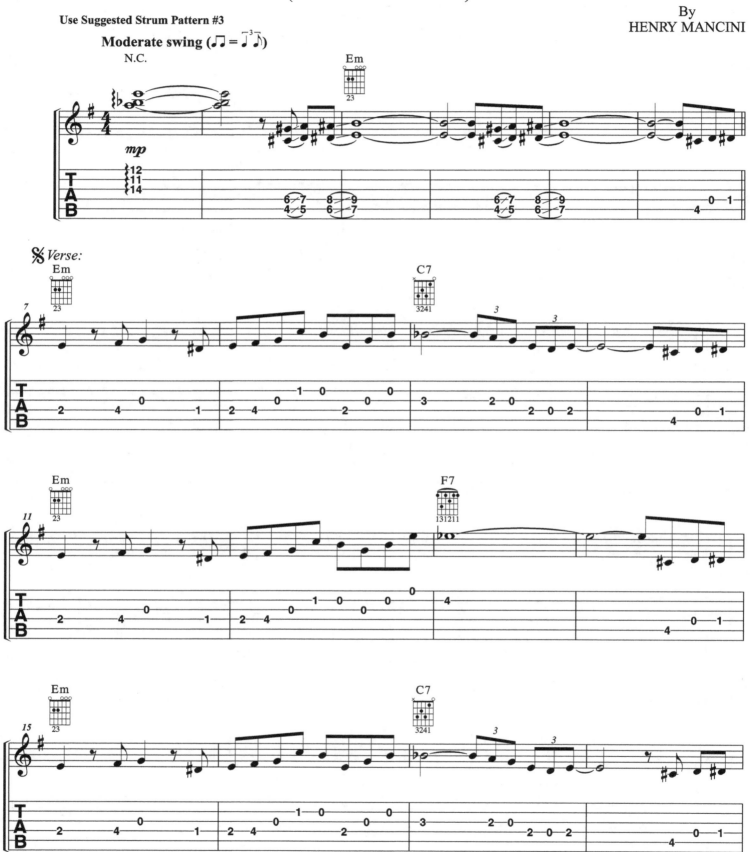

The Pink Panther - 3 - 1

The Pink Panther - 3 - 2

120

The Pink Panther - 3 - 3

# THE PRAYER

Words and Music by
CAROLE BAYER SAGER
and DAVID FOSTER

The Prayer - 3 - 1

# SINGIN' IN THE RAIN

Lyric by
ARTHUR FREED

Music by
NACIO HERB BROWN

126

Singin' in the Rain - 3 - 3

# SOMEWHERE, MY LOVE
# (LARA'S THEME)
### (from *Doctor Zhivago*)

Lyric by
PAUL FRANCIS WEBSTER

Music by
MAURICE JARRE

**Use Suggested Strum Pattern #9**
**or Fingerpicking Pattern #13**
**Moderately fast but gentle waltz ♩ = 180**

*Verse 1:*

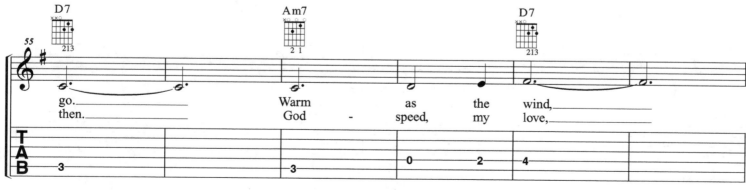

Somewhere, My Love (Lara's Theme) - 3 - 3

# THE SUMMER KNOWS
## (Theme from *The Summer of '42*)

Lyrics by
**ALAN and MARILYN BERGMAN**

Music by
**MICHEL LEGRAND**

**Use Suggested Strum Pattern #6
or Fingerpicking Pattern #4**

**Slowly** ♩ = 60

The Summer Knows - 2 - 1

sun to lin - ger. Twists the world 'round her sum - mer fin - ger, lets you see the

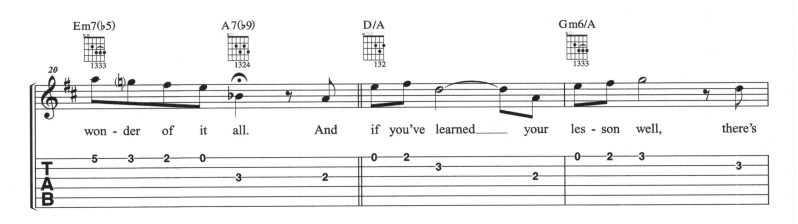

won - der of it all. And if you've learned____ your les - son well, there's

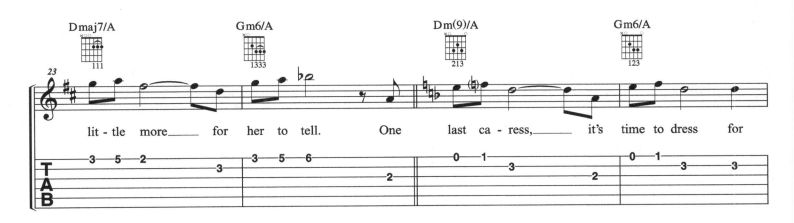

lit - tle more____ for her to tell. One last ca - ress,____ it's time to dress for

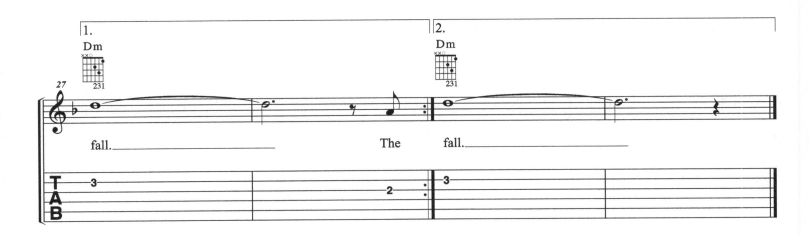

1.
fall._____

2.
The fall._____

# THEME FROM *ICE CASTLES*
## (Through the Eyes of Love)

Lyrics by
**CAROLE BAYER SAGER**

Music by
**MARVIN HAMLISCH**

**Use Suggested Strum Pattern #7**

**Slowly, with expression** ♩ = 69

1. Please, don't let this feel-ing end. It's ev-'ry-thing I am, ev-'ry-thing I want to be. I can see what's mine now, find-ing out what's true much } since I found you look-ing through the eyes of love. 2. And

(2.) now I can take the time. I can see my life as it comes up shin-ing now. Reach-ing out to touch you, I can feel so so much }

3. Please, don't let this feel-ing end. It might not come a-gain, and I want to re-mem-ber how it feels to touch you, how I feel so so much }

*To Coda* ⊕

Theme from *Ice Castles* (Through the Eyes of Love) - 2 - 1

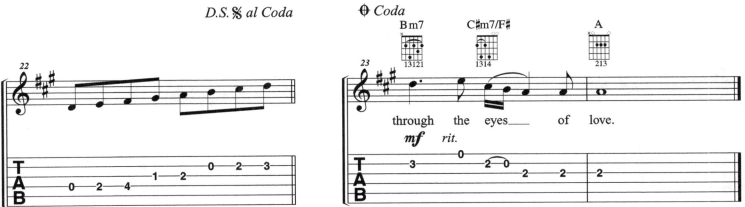

# TALK TO THE ANIMALS

(from *Doctor Doolittle*)

**Use Suggested Strum Pattern #14**

Words and Music by
LESLIE BRICUSSE

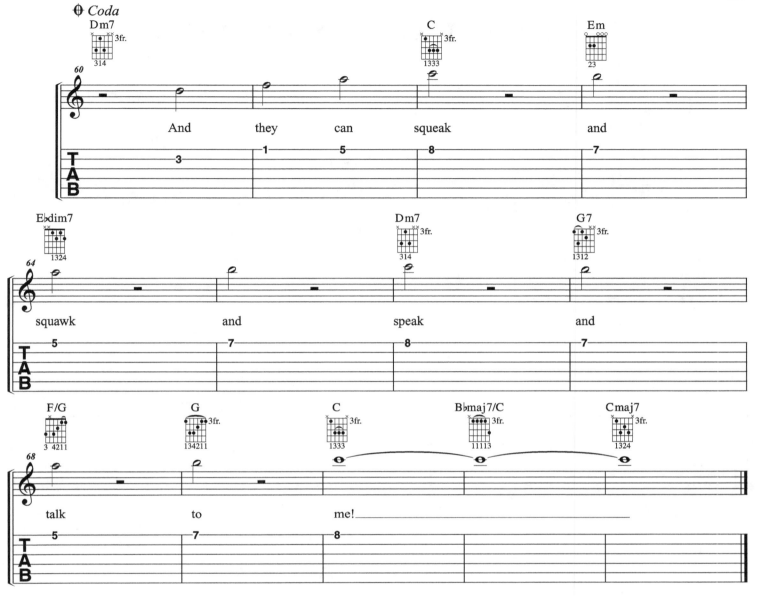

**Verse 2:**
If I could talk to the animals,
Learn their languages,
Maybe take an animal degree.
I'd study elephant and eagle,
Buffalo and beagle,
Alligator, guinea pig and flea.
*(To Bridge1:)*

**Verse 4:**
If I could talk to the animals,
Think what fun I'd have asking over crocodiles for tea.
Or maybe lunch with two or three lions,
Walruses and sea lions,
What a lovely place the world would be.

**Verse 5:**
If I spoke slang to orangutangs, the advantages,
Any fool on earth can plainly see.
Discussing eastern art and dramas
With intellectual llamas.
That's a big step forward, you'll agree.

**Bridge 2:**
I'd learn to speak in antelope and turtle.
My Pekinese would be extremely good.
If I were asked to sing in hippopotamus,
I'd say, "Why notamus?" And would.

**Verse 6:**
If I could parlay with pachyderms,
It's a fairy tale worthy of Hans Andersen or Grimm.
The man who walks with the animals,
Talks with the animals,
Grunts and squeaks and squawks with the animals,
And they can talk to him.

**Bridge 3:**
I'd study ev'ry living creature's language,
So I could speak to all of them on sight.
If friends say, "Can he talk in crab or pelican?"
You'll say, "Like hellican!"
And you'd be right.

**Verse 7:**
And if you just stop to think a bit,
There's no doubt of it,
I will have a place in history.
For I can walk with the cats and dogs,
Talk with the toads and frogs,
Grunt and squeak and squawk with the pig and hogs.
And they can squeak and squawk and speak and talk to me!

# THE SOUND OF SILENCE

Words and Music by
PAUL SIMON

The Sound of Silence - 3 - 1

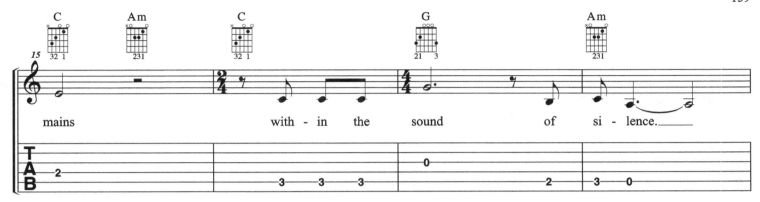

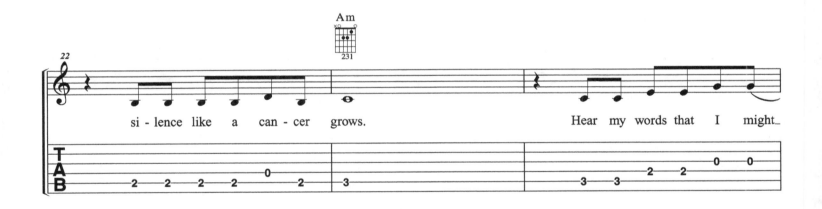

The Sound of Silence - 3 - 2

Verse 2:
In restless dreams I walked alone, narrow streets of cobblestone.
'Neath the halo of a streetlamp I turned my collar to the cold and damp,
When my eyes were stabbed by the flash of a neon light
That split the night and touched the sound of silence.

Verse 3:
And in the naked light I saw ten thousand people, maybe more.
People talking without speaking, people hearing without list'ning.
People writing songs that voices never share
And no one dared disturb the sound of silence.
(To Verse 4:)

Verse 5:
And the people bowed and prayed to the neon god they made.
And the sign flashed out its warning in the words that it was forming.
And the sign said, "The words of the prophets are written on the subway walls
And tenement halls" and whispered in the sounds of silence.

# THEME FROM *NEW YORK, NEW YORK*

Words by
FRED EBB

Music by
JOHN KANDER

**Use Suggested Strum Pattern #14**

Moderate swing

Theme from *New York, New York* - 3 - 2

Theme from *New York, New York* - 3 - 3

# THEME FROM *PEYTON PLACE*

Lyrics by
PAUL FRANCIS WEBSTER

Music by
FRANZ WAXMAN

**Use Suggested Strum Pattern #9**

**Moderately slow waltz**

Theme from *Peyton Place* - 2 - 1

Theme from *Peyton Place* - 2 - 2

# THEME FROM *ZORBA THE GREEK*
## (Zorba's Dance)

By
MIKIS THEODORAKIS

**Use Suggested Strum Pattern #14 or Fingerpicking Pattern #15**

**Slowly (speed up as indicated throughout)**

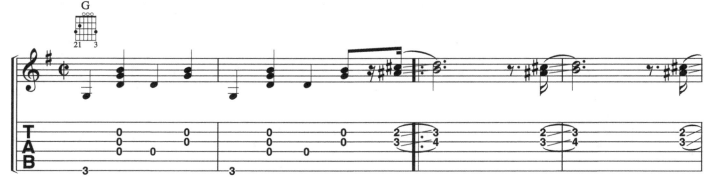

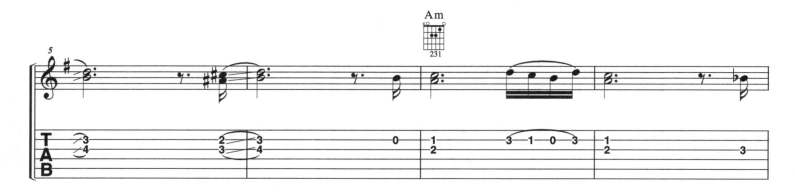

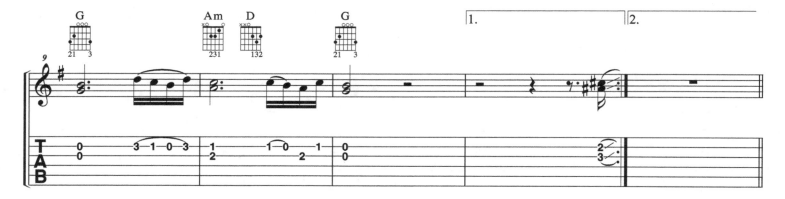

**A little faster**

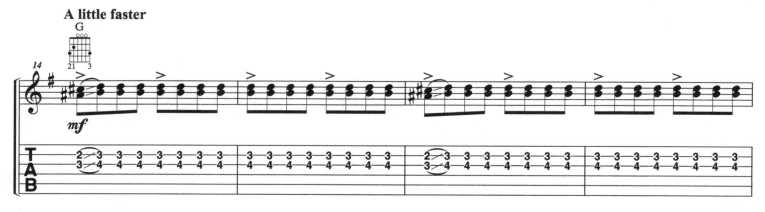

Theme from *Zorba the Greek* - 4 - 1

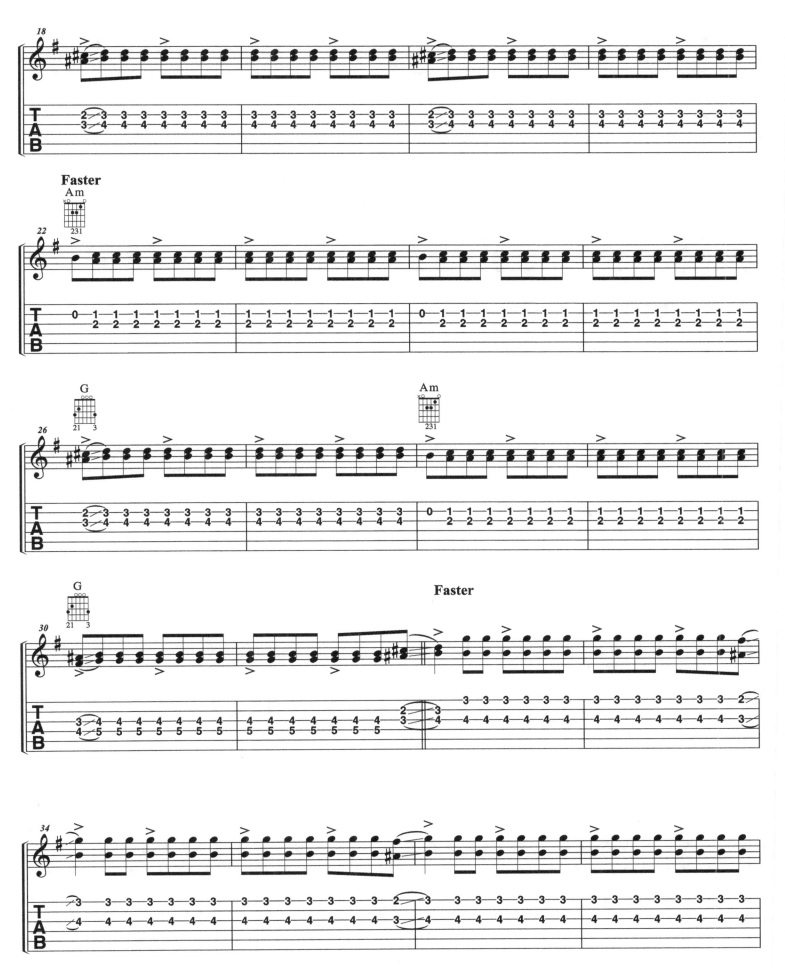

Theme from *Zorba the Greek* - 4 - 2

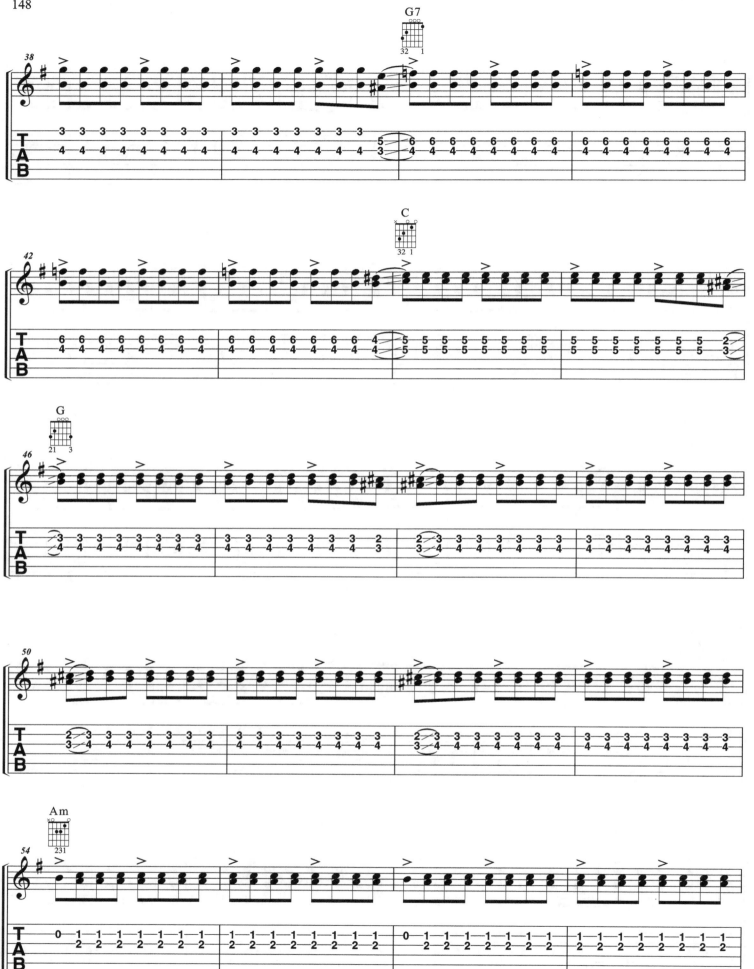

Theme from *Zorba the Greek* - 4 - 4

# WE BELONG TOGETHER

(from *Toy Story 3*)

Words and Music by
RANDY NEWMAN

Use Intro or Rhythm Slashes as Suggested Strum Pattern

**Moderately bright**

We Belong Together - 4 - 1

# THE WINDMILLS OF YOUR MIND

(from *The Thomas Crown Affair*)

Words by
ALAN and MARILYN BERGMAN

Music by
MICHEL LEGRAND

The Windmills of Your Mind - 5 - 1

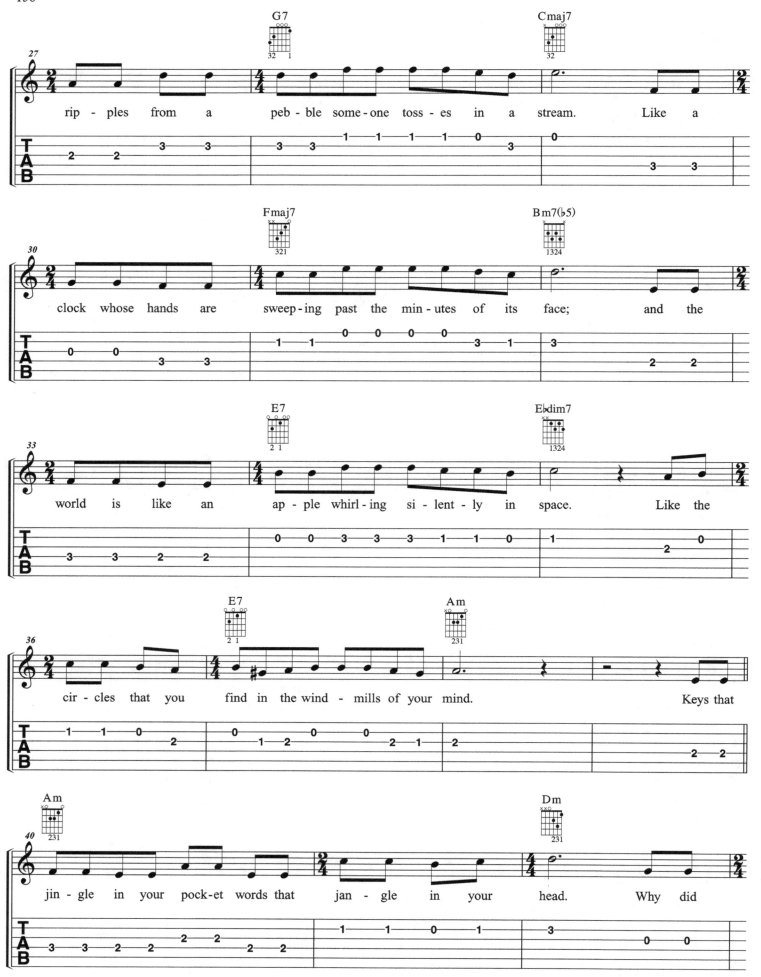

# WHAT ARE YOU DOING
# THE REST OF YOUR LIFE?

Lyrics by
ALAN AND MARILYN BERGMAN

Music by
MICHEL LEGRAND

**Use Suggested Strum Pattern #3
or Fingerpicking Pattern #4**

**Slowly ♩ = 70**

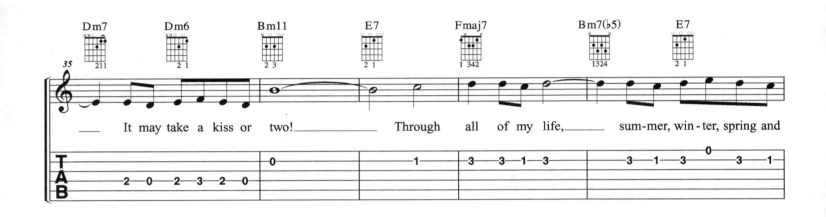

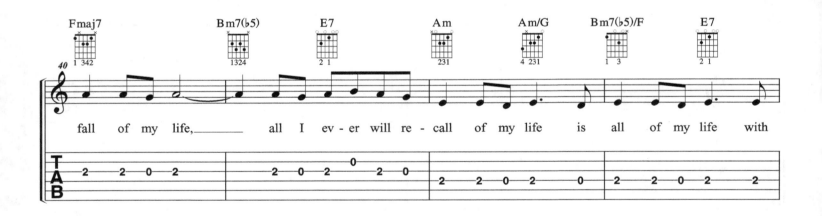

What Are You Doing the Rest of Your Life? - 3 - 3

# WHAT'S NEW PUSSYCAT?

Words by
HAL DAVID

Music by
BURT BACHARACH

**Use Suggested Strum Pattern #9**

**Bright waltz** (♫ = ♪³♪)

*Chorus:*

What's new, Pus-sy-cat? Whoa.___

What's new, Pus-sy-cat? Whoa.___

oh.___

*Verse:*

1. Pus - sy - cat, Pus - sy - cat, I've got flow - ers and
2. Pus - sy - cat, Pus - sy - cat, you're so thrill - ing and
3. Pus - sy - cat, Pus - sy - cat, you're de - li - cious and,

What's New Pussycat? - 4 - 1

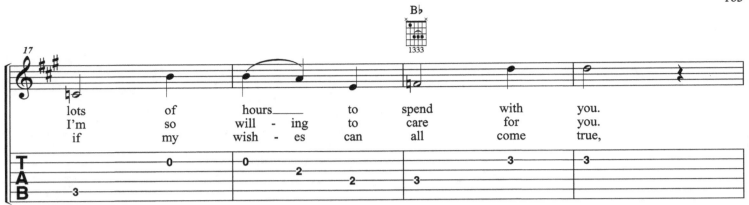

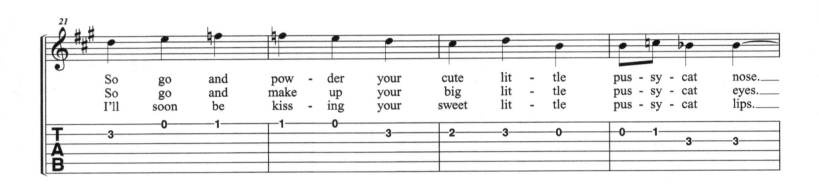

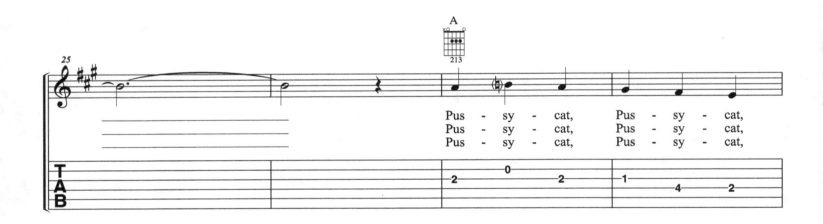

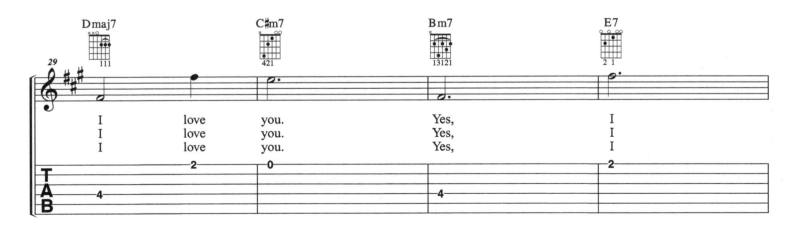

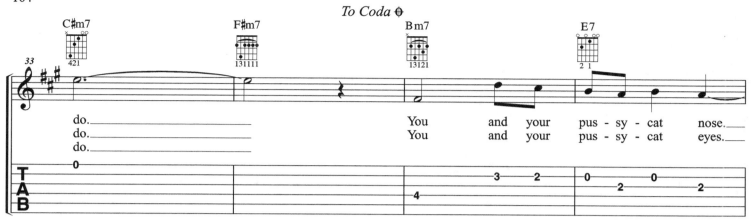

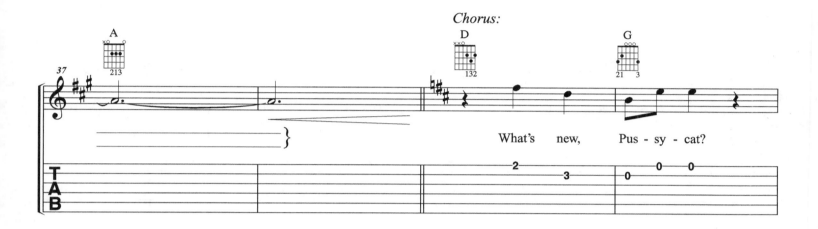

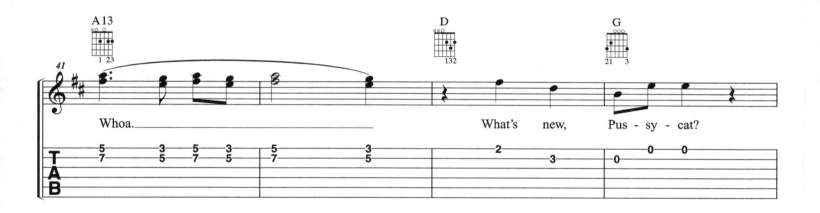

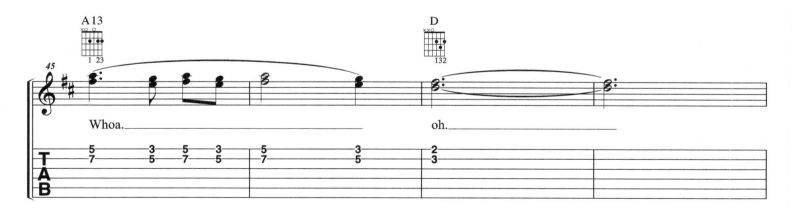

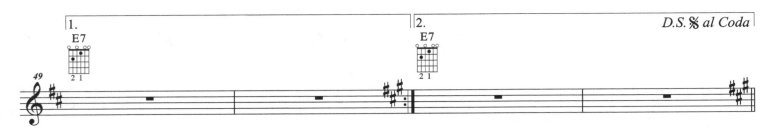

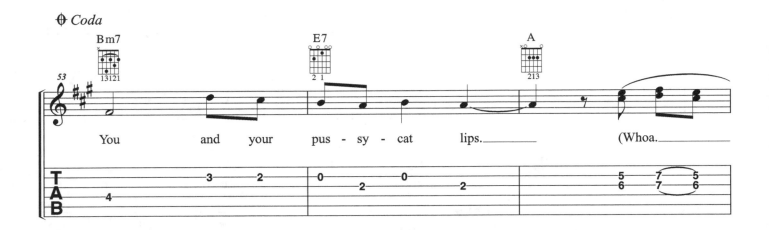

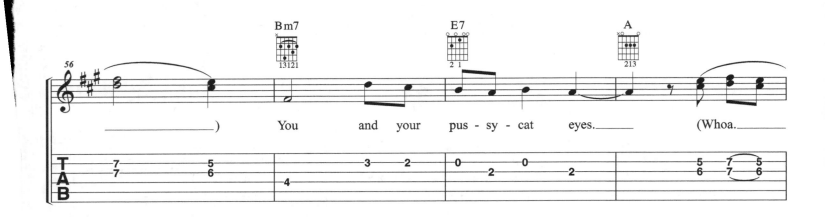

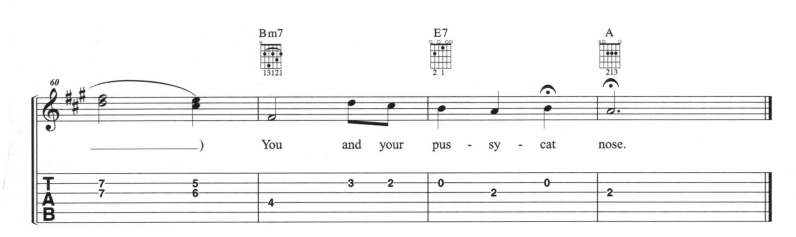

What's New Pussycat? - 4 - 4

# YOU'VE GOT A FRIEND IN ME

(from *Toy Story*)

**Use Suggested Strum Pattern #14
or Fingerpick simile to Intro**

Words and Music by
RANDY NEWMAN

**Moderate swing**

*Verses 1 & 2:*

1. You've got a friend in me.____ You've got a friend in me.____
2. *See additional lyrics*

____ When the road____ looks rough a - head____ and you're miles____

____ and miles____ from your nice____ warm bed.____ You just re - mem - ber what your

You've Got a Friend in Me - 3 - 1

You've Got a Friend in Me - 3 - 2

*Verse 2:*
You've got a friend in me.
You've got a friend in me.
You got troubles, then I got 'em too.
There isn't anything I would-n't do for you.
If we stick together we can see it through,
'Cause you've got a friend in me.
*(To Bridge:)*